IT'S MY STATE!

ILLINOIS

Claire Price-Groff

Elizabeth Kaplan

Marshall Cavendish
Benchmark
New York

Published by Marshall Cavendish Benchmark
An imprint of Marshall Cavendish Corporation

Website: www.marshallcavendish.us

This publication represents the opinions and views of the authors based on their personal experience, knowledge, and research. The information in this book serves as a general guide only. The authors and publisher have used their best efforts in preparing this book and disclaim liability rising directly and indirectly from the use and application of this book.

Other Marshall Cavendish Offices:
Marshall Cavendish International (Asia) Private Limited, 1 New Industrial Road, Singapore 536196 •
Marshall Cavendish International (Thailand) Co Ltd. 253 Asoke, 12th Flr, Sukhumvit 21 Road, Klongtoey Nua, Wattana, Bangkok 10110, Thailand • Marshall Cavendish (Malaysia) Sdn Bhd, Times Subang, Lot 46, Subang Hi-Tech Industrial Park, Batu Tiga, 40000 Shah Alam, Selangor Darul Ehsan, Malaysia

Marshall Cavendish is a trademark of Times Publishing Limited

All websites were available and accurate when this book was sent to press.

Library of Congress Cataloging-in-Publication Data
Price-Groff, Claire.
          Illinois / Claire Price-Groff, Elizabeth Kaplan. — 2nd ed.
                 p. cm. — (It's my state!)
          Includes index.
          ISBN 978-1-60870-050-9
          1. Illinois—Juvenile literature. I. Kaplan, Elizabeth, 1956-
          II. Title.
     F541.3.P75 2011
     977.3—dc22   2010003923

Second Edition developed for Marshall Cavendish Benchmark by RJF Publishing LLC (www.RJFpublishing.com)
Series Designer, Second Edition: Tammy West/Westgraphix LLC
Editor, Second Edition: Brian Fitzgerald

All maps, illustrations, and graphics © Marshall Cavendish Corporation. Maps and artwork on pages 6, 32, 33, 75, and back cover by Christopher Santoro. Map and graphics on pages 8 and 43 by Westgraphix LLC. Map on page 76 by Mapping Specialists.

The photographs in this book are used by permission and through the courtesy of:
Front cover: Vito Palmisano/Getty Images and Kathryn Russell Studios/Getty Images (inset).
Alamy: Bill Brooks, 17 (bottom); North Wind Picture Archives, 22, 29, 30 (left); Chuck Eckert, 40; Charles O. Cecil, 49; Flame, 50; Jason Lindsey, 51; Jim West, 56; Kim Karpeles, 57, 73, 74; Joseph Jarosz, 60; AGStockUSA, 62. *The Bridgeman Art Library:* Peter Newark American Pictures: The British surrender Vincennes to George Rogers Clark in 1779 (colour litho) by H. Charles Jr. McBarron (1902-92) (after) Private Collection, 24. *Corbis:* Bettmann, 31, 46. *The Field Museum:* © 1987 GEO85129c, 5 (bottom). *Getty Images:* Gay Bumgarner, 4; Gail Shumway, 5 (top); Greg Neise, 9; Altrendo Nature, 10 (top); James L. Stanfield, 10 (bottom); Amanda Hall , 11; Win McNamee, 12; Willard Clay 14 (top), 71 (top); John E. Marriott, 14 (bottom); Jeff Foott, 16; Wallace Kirkland, 18; University/AFP, 21; Hulton Archive, 27; National Archives, 28; Robert Harding Productions, 30 (right); Chicago History Museum/Hulton Archive, 34; Buyenlarge/Hulton Archive, 35; Charles Fenno Jacobs/Time & Life Pictures, 36; Juan Silva, 38; Tim Boyle, 41; Jeff Haynes/AFP, 44; Nathaniel S. Butler/NBAE, 45; Johnny Nunez/Wire Image, 47 (top); Joe Scherschel/National Geographic, 52, 71 (bottom); Ray Laskowitz, 55; Scott Olson, 59, 64; Jetta Productions, 63; Scott Boehm, 67; Michael L. Abramson/Time Life Pictures, 69; Wesley Hitt, 70. *Museum of Science and Industry:* Charlie Westerman, 72. *Photo Researchers Inc.:* Larry L. Miller, 17 (top). *Shutterstock:* Thomas Barrat, 13. *U.S. Fish and Wildlife Service:* 15. *White House Photo:* Pete Souza, 47 (bottom).

Printed in Malaysia (T).
135642

CONTENTS

State Flower: Purple Violet

Known for the delicate beauty of its purple blossoms, the violet was chosen as the state flower by Illinois schoolchildren in 1907.

State Tree: White Oak

Young Illinoisans chose this acorn-bearing tree as their state tree in 1973. In the fall, the tree's leaves change color, creating a beautiful display of orange, red, and yellow.

State Bird: Cardinal

In the past, these brightly colored birds visited the state only in spring and summer. Today, they are year-round residents.

State Fish: Bluegill

Easy to spot because of the bluish color of its gills, the bluegill became the state fish in 1986. Bluegills can be found throughout the state. These small sunfish are only about 9 inches (23 centimeters) long but are very popular fish to catch.

State Insect: Monarch Butterfly

Schoolchildren proposed this orange-and-black butterfly as the state insect in 1974. The monarch butterfly's bold color is actually a warning to other animals that it would make a very bad-tasting meal.

State Fossil: Tully Monster

About 300 million years ago, this soft-bodied sea animal thrived. First discovered by Francis Tully in 1958, Tully monster fossils are all over Illinois—more than a hundred have been found.

1
The Prairie State

Illinoisans like to think of their state as the center of the nation's heartland. In different parts of the state, ancient cypress swamps and majestic river cliffs fill the landscape. You might see riverboats gliding over the smooth waters of the major rivers that pass around and through Illinois. You can find peaceful prairies with rolling fields of wheat and herds of grazing cattle. Also running through this heartland are the many highways and roads that lead from the farmland toward the big cities and their surrounding areas, called suburbs. From bustling cities to quiet prairies, Illinois seems to have it all.

Illinois looks kind of like a giant key. It is the twenty-fourth largest state and covers 55,584 square miles (143,962 square kilometers). The state has 102 counties. Chicago, the state's largest city, is in Cook County. It has the second-highest population of any county in the United States. Springfield, the state capital, is in Sangamon County in the central part of the state.

The Landscape
Different types of terrain make up the northwestern section of the state. That is where you will find Illinois's highest points and deepest valleys. The hilly prairies are broken up by jagged

Quick Facts

ILLINOIS BORDERS

North	Wisconsin
South	Kentucky
East	Indiana
West	Iowa
	Missouri

Illinois Counties

Illinois has 102 counties.

This tallgrass prairie lies in the north-central part of Illinois.

limestone cliffs and rocky outcrops. The northwestern portion of the state also has wetlands, forests, and marshes.

The northeast has rich plains dotted with small lakes and marshes. Much of the farmland that once covered the region has given way to cities. Chicago is located in the eastern section of those plains. The southern end of Lake Michigan serves as the northeastern border of the state.

The central portion of Illinois boasts some of the most fertile soil in the United States. Much of the area is flat land that is perfect for farming. But gently rolling hills also add variety to the landscape. The hills were created millions of years ago when glaciers—large bodies of ice—moved across the earth, bringing rich soil to the region. The glaciers also carved high ridges, deep canyons, and caves across south-central Illinois. The soil in the south-central part of the state, however, is mostly clay and is not good for farming.

The western portion of Illinois, between the Illinois and Mississippi rivers, has many hills, valleys, small lakes, and streams. This west-central area of the state is perfect for people who love fishing and boating. It is also a wonderful area for mountain biking. Many miles of trails have been developed to help people enjoy that sport.

To the south are the Illinois Ozarks, a hilly region that has impressive sandstone cliffs and deep canyons. Unlike much of the more-level Illinois

The unique rock formations in the Garden of the Gods wilderness area are more than 300 million years old.

landscape, this rugged terrain was not created by glaciers. The Shawnee National Forest stretches across the region, covering more than 250,000 acres (101,170 hectares). The only national forest in Illinois, it is a popular place for hiking, camping, canoeing, and horseback riding. Within the Shawnee National Forest is the Garden of the Gods wilderness area. Large rock formations, sculpted by the wind into interesting shapes, give this part of the forest its name. Hikers in the Garden of the Gods can see rocks in unusual shapes, including a camel, a mushroom, a smokestack, and a table.

The southern part of the state is bounded by two large rivers, the Ohio and the Mississippi. This region is sometimes called Egypt or Little Egypt. One explanation for these nicknames is that the majestic rivers made early European-American settlers think of the Nile River in Egypt. The southernmost city in Illinois is Cairo (in Illinois pronounced CARE-oh), which is named after that famous Egyptian city.

Waterways

Several bodies of water form the state's borders. The

The sun begins to set over Cairo, Illinois, where the Mississippi and Ohio rivers meet.

This view of Lake Michigan shows the Chicago skyline in the distance.

Mississippi River cuts western Illinois into a series of notches as it flows south. Lake Michigan, one of the five Great Lakes, sits at the state's northeast corner. The Wabash River separates southeastern Illinois from Indiana. The Ohio River forms the border between southern Illinois and Kentucky. The Illinois River drains a large area across the central portion of the state. Almost all the rivers in Illinois, large or small, eventually flow into the Mississippi. Many of these rivers are great for fishing, which is a popular sport throughout Illinois.

Illinois's most important port city is Chicago on Lake Michigan. Lake Michigan is the sixth-largest freshwater lake in the world. A person standing on its shore cannot see across it to the opposite side. Illinois has several other large lakes, including Carlyle Lake and Rend Lake. Like most of the state's larger lakes, they were created when a dam was built across a river.

Illinois's many lakes and rivers are important both to the state's economy and to its wildlife. Commercial boats and barges commonly carry farm products and manufactured items to Illinois's ports. The goods are then shipped to the rest of the country and all over the world. Pleasure boats also cruise and fish the lakes

The 2008 Mississippi River flood wiped out this farm in Quincy, Illinois.

and rivers. And many types of birds, fish, and other wildlife make their homes in the state's waterways.

Climate

Long, cold winters and hot, humid summers are common in northern Illinois. Almost every year, Chicago newspaper headlines report illnesses or deaths related to weather extremes. In the winter, it is common for the temperature to dip well below 0 degrees Fahrenheit (–17 degrees Celsius). In the summer, it is equally common for the temperature to rise well above 90 °F (32 °C).

In the spring and early summer, the Mississippi and other rivers in Illinois sometimes overflow, causing floods in the lowlands along the rivers. In 1993, thousands of people in the western part of the state lost farms, homes, and businesses to floods. The flooding was the worst in Illinois history. Severe flooding again occurred on the Mississippi and other rivers throughout central Illinois in 2008. People in Illinois and other states along the Mississippi River are working to learn more about the causes of severe flooding. This will help Illinoisans and others live more safely along these flowing waterways.

Severe thunderstorms are not uncommon in Illinois. With these storms comes the threat of tornadoes, especially in the spring and summer. A tornado is a swirling column of air that stretches from a storm cloud all the way to the ground. In a tornado, wind speeds can reach more than 200 miles (320 km) per hour. Tornadoes can form very quickly and cause huge amounts of damage—uprooting trees, ripping off roofs, and tossing cars into the air.

Despite the sometimes harsh weather, Illinoisans appreciate their state's varied climate. Many people love to watch their state change with the seasons—the burst of new life in spring, the full bloom of summer, the glorious colors of fall, and the beauty of freshly fallen snow in winter.

Skaters enjoy a winter day at a skating rink in downtown Chicago.

Quick Facts

FARMERS AND CONSERVATION

Some farmers in Illinois are not planting food crops. Instead they are planting trees for forests and wild grasses for prairies. Much of the land had been seriously eroded, or worn away, when it was farmed. One farmer described the gullies on his farm as deep enough to completely hold a car. Now this land is being managed to attract and feed wildlife. In addition, replanting the land with native grasses and trees helps prevent water pollution and flooding.

Lush plant life covers the floor of the Ryerson Conservation Area in Riverwoods, Illinois.

Wildlife

Not only farm crops grow well in Illinois—so do many wildflowers, grasses, and trees. Purple violets, lilies, bluebells, hyacinths, marsh marigolds, and other wildflowers sprinkle the roadsides and fields with color in spring and summer. The brilliant reds and yellows of changing leaves paint the landscape in fall.

In the past, more than half the state was covered with forests of ash, cottonwood, elm, hickory, and oak. Today, only about 12 percent of Illinois land is forested. More than two-thirds of Illinois's original forests were cut down by European-American settlers who plowed the land and planted crops. Other forests were cleared to build towns and cities. Today, the most heavily forested part of the state lies in the south, within the Shawnee National Forest.

A variety of animals and birds are native to Illinois. The white-tailed deer—the state's official animal—is the biggest animal in Illinois. Rabbits, squirrels, muskrats, skunks, raccoons, foxes, and mink scamper through

White-tailed deer are a familiar sight in wooded areas throughout the state.

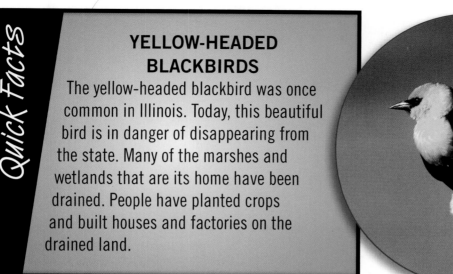

YELLOW-HEADED BLACKBIRDS

The yellow-headed blackbird was once common in Illinois. Today, this beautiful bird is in danger of disappearing from the state. Many of the marshes and wetlands that are its home have been drained. People have planted crops and built houses and factories on the drained land.

the forests. Ducks, quail, grouse, and pheasant nest and feed along the state's waterways and in fields. Huge flocks of Canada geese darken the skies in the spring. They are returning from a winter spent farther south and are stopping in Illinois to build nests, lay eggs, and hatch their young. Thousands of Canada geese also live year-round throughout the state. The birds create problems by destroying crops and fouling lakes and ponds. However, they are a protected species and can be hunted only during specific times of the year. Many birds make their homes in the trees of Illinois. Cardinals and other songbirds sing out from the treetops. Bald eagles watch for prey while perched on high.

Threatened Wildlife

Several kinds of animals that were once common in Illinois have become extinct. Other animals are currently in danger of dying out. Among Illinois's endangered animals are fish, including several species of sturgeons and chubs. Certain types of turtles, snakes, and salamanders could completely disappear. Pollution and the loss of forests have put species of hawks, owls, songbirds, and shore birds and several small woods and prairie animals at risk of losing their natural homes. Many other animals and numerous plants are endangered in Illinois and are likely to become extinct unless people make a strong effort to save them.

Fox Squirrel

The fox squirrel lives mostly at the edge of forests or woodlands. It is good at moving from tree to tree and can jump nearly 18 feet (5.5 meters).

Bobcat

A bobcat may look like some house cats, but it can weigh up to 40 pounds (18 kilograms). This cat is named for its short—"bobbed"—tail that is only about 5 inches (12.7 cm) long. For more than one hundred years, the number of bobcats in Illinois was very low. In the past few decades, however, bobcat populations have been growing. Bobcats are now found in all parts of the state.

Coyote

Coyotes usually hunt at night, roaming an area as wide as 30 miles (48 km). They are swift runners, reaching speeds of more than 40 miles (64 km) per hour. That is faster than the speed limit on most Illinois city streets. Coyotes are common in Illinois and are becoming increasingly common in suburban and urban areas.

Red Bat

The tiny red bat weighs less than 1 ounce (30 grams) and is only one of twelve kinds of bats found in Illinois. The red bat gets its name from its brownish-red fur. But each hair has a white tip, so this bat could easily be nicknamed the frosted bat. Red bats live mostly in trees. Unlike many other types of bats, red bats do not live in large groups, or colonies.

Wild Blue Iris

These beautiful flowers bloom in early spring. In Illinois they can be found along the shores of ponds and small lakes, in marshes, and in wet parts of prairies.

Goldenglow Flower

These brilliant-yellow, daisylike flowers dot Illinois roadsides in midsummer.

From the Beginning

What do the frozen plains of Siberia in northern Asia have to do with Illinois? Scientists believe that between 10,000 and 30,000 years ago, the Bering Sea—the stretch of water between Alaska and eastern Siberia—did not exist. Sea levels were lower then, and land that is now under the Bering Sea was above water, creating a land bridge between the two continents. Most anthropologists (scientists who study different cultures, including ancient cultures) think a few brave, strong people crossed that bridge. If this is true, the many tribes of American Indians that spread across the Americas are the descendants of those adventurers.

The earliest people to live in the area now called Illinois were nomadic groups that moved from place to place hunting large game. Later people who lived in the region hunted smaller game and gathered wild grains and edible roots, bulbs, berries, and nuts. Eventually, the region's natives began to grow grain instead of gathering it where it grew wild. They ground the grain into coarse flour for cooking and baking.

Quick Facts

HUNTING MASTODONS

Mastodons—large, furry mammals similar to elephants—once lived in North America. In western Illinois, scientists have found 11,000-year-old mastodon bones with cut marks. The bones are evidence that prehistoric hunters lived in the region.

A young girl stands in front of a huge corn crib. Farming has played a key role in the history and growth of Illinois.

The First Settlements

Over time, ancient people in what is now Illinois learned more about the food plants whose seeds they collected and scattered each year. They learned where the plants grew best and decided to stay in these areas year-round. About three thousand years ago, they began building permanent settlements, mostly in river valleys.

Even before they built year-round settlements, the ancient Illinoisans had buried some members of their groups in earthen mounds. Over the centuries, they built larger and more complex mounds. By about 100 BCE, mound building had become an important part of the culture of many peoples living in the American Midwest.

Cities on the Mississippi

About 700 CE, people in Illinois began growing corn as a main food source. It was a more reliable source of food than other crops. The cultivation of corn led to growth in the population and to the development of a distinctive culture. Because most of the people lived along the Mississippi or other rivers flowing into the Mississippi, the culture is called the Mississippian culture.

In Mississippian culture, small villages surrounded large towns or cities. At the center of most towns and cities was a large, flat mound with a temple or a leader's home built on top. The largest of the Mississippian cities was Cahokia, in southwestern Illinois. The city served as a cultural center for centuries. About 20,000 people lived in Cahokia when the city was at its peak.

Over the next 250 years, Cahokia's population declined. By 1400, very few people lived in Cahokia and in other large Mississippian villages in present-day Illinois. This may have been because the climate was getting colder, which led

This drawing shows what the human-made earthen structure called Monks Mound looked like in the 1880s. This mound was part of the Cahokia civilization, which disappeared more than 600 years ago.

to poor harvests. Overpopulation, disease, and invasion might have also added to the problems.

By the 1600s, two main groups of American Indians had come to live in what today is Illinois. One group was the Miami, who built villages south and west of Lake Michigan. By the 1700s, the Miami had moved to present-day eastern Indiana. The other group was the Illinois (also called the Illiniwek), who lived throughout the central Mississippi River valley. Both groups spoke similar Algonquian languages.

Quick Facts

THE TRIBES OF ILLINOIS

In the mid–1700s, the Illinois Indians included five tribes: the Cahokia, Kaskaskia, Peoria, Michigamea, and Tamaroa. The first four have lent their names to important places in the state of Illinois and in the Midwest. The descendants of these tribes are represented by one tribe today— the Peoria, whose headquarters is in Oklahoma.

The First European Settlers

In 1673, the French government in New France (part of present-day Canada) was looking for new trade routes. Louis Jolliet and Jacques Marquette were chosen to explore the river that the Algonquian-speakers called *Misi sipi*, or "big river." They wanted to see if the river stretched west to the Pacific Ocean. Louis Jolliet was a French Canadian who had been exploring the Great Lakes region for New France. Jacques Marquette was a French priest who had worked and lived among the

This drawing shows Jacques Marquette, Louis Jolliet, and their American Indian guides exploring the Upper Mississippi River in 1673.

American Indians and could speak a number of Indian languages. In May 1673, Marquette and Jolliet launched canoes at the northern edge of Lake Michigan and began their journey southward.

Marquette and Jolliet paddled along the shores of Lake Michigan and then traveled down rivers in what is today Wisconsin. They eventually reached the Mississippi River. They followed it as far south as present-day Arkansas. They also traveled north, along the Illinois River. A year later, Marquette returned to the banks of the Illinois River to establish a mission (a religious settlement) at an Indian village called Kaskaskia, which later became the town of Utica.

The French claimed the area that Marquette and Jolliet explored, naming it Illinois, after the Indians who lived there. In the early 1700s, the French considered Illinois part of their province of Louisiana—a vast area that included nearly the entire midsection of North America. The first permanent European settlement in Illinois was established in the town of Cahokia in 1699.

Many European settlements were established on North America's east coast. But over time, European colonists began to move west. As a result, Indian tribes were pushed westward from their homelands.

Despite their differences, Europeans and Indians traded with each other. Indians exchanged animal skins for the Europeans' metal tools, horses, and guns. But the European settlers also brought new diseases to North America. American Indians had never been exposed to these illnesses and had no resistance to them. As a result, thousands of Indians died.

The arrival of more Europeans took its toll on the land. Settlers chopped down forests and hunted animals for food and their skins. Indians could no longer find the animals they needed for food. In self-defense, they learned to use their horses and guns to fight back against the Europeans. But more European colonists kept coming. The Indians were fighting a hopeless battle.

The European settlers also fought each other. The British and French competed for control of North America. During the French and Indian War (1754–1763), both the British and French armies were aided by American Indian allies. The British won the war and gained control of Illinois and most other

French territory in North America east of the Mississippi River. Still, most white people in Illinois at that time were French.

The American Revolution in Illinois

By the 1770s, many colonists along the eastern coast of North America wanted to break free from British control. The Thirteen Colonies approved the Declaration of Independence on July 4, 1776, but freedom did not come easily. First, the colonists had to fight and win the American Revolution.

Most battles were fought in the colonies, but some fighting took place in Illinois. The most important battle was on July 4, 1778. American forces led by George Rogers Clark captured the British forts at Kaskaskia, as well as Cahokia

This painting shows the British surrendering one of their forts to George Rogers Clark in 1779.

and several other small towns. In his journal Clark wrote, "In the evening, we got within a few miles of the town, where we lay until near dark. . . . In a very little time we had complete possession." He claimed all the territory north of the Ohio River as part of the newly formed United States. Clark's victory at Kaskaskia also persuaded local French residents to fight on the American side.

The Illinois Territory

The American colonists eventually won their independence. In the 1783 treaty ending the American Revolution, the United States also got from Great Britain a huge area of land to the west of the Thirteen Colonies. Almost all the land between the former colonies and the Mississippi River became part of the new United States. The area north of the Ohio River, including Illinois, was called the Northwest Territory. In 1800, the part of the Northwest Territory that included present-day Illinois was renamed the Indiana Territory. Nine years later, the district split. Part of the district became the Illinois Territory, which included present-day Illinois, Wisconsin, and Michigan.

In the early 1800s, Americans of European descent started moving into present-day Illinois in large numbers. They built cabins and chopped through the tough prairie sod (grass-covered soil) to plant crops. Their new land was good for farming, but their lives were not easy. Many items these settlers had taken for granted in their previous homes were not available. They had to make most of their own goods or do without them.

Illinois officially became the twenty-first state on December 3, 1818. By 1830, the state's population had grown to more than 160,000 people. As more settlers arrived, the Indians were forced to move west.

Quick Facts

THE CLARK BROTHERS

George Rogers Clark was an early pioneer. He spent several years exploring what is now Kentucky and doing land surveys there. His younger brother William was a leader of the Lewis and Clark expedition. William helped explore the northwestern part of the United States in the early 1800s.

Some American Indians refused to leave their homelands. In 1832, Black Hawk, a leader among the Sauk and Fox tribes, tried to take back tribal land in northern Illinois and Wisconsin. He and his warriors fought bravely, but they were badly outnumbered and were quickly defeated. President Andrew Jackson sent Black Hawk and his son Whirling Thunder around the country as "trophies" of war. The two men behaved with such dignity that they gained much admiration. Black Hawk returned to his people on a reservation in Iowa, where he wrote his autobiography.

Throughout the period, the United States government signed pacts and treaties with Indian tribes. The government took away the lands where the Indians had always lived and gave them other land farther west. But as European-American settlers moved toward the Pacific coast, the United States broke many of those treaties.

In Their Own Words

We didn't have any coffee, but we had some tea that we raised in the garden called "sage" tea.... The sugar we had was maple sugar, that we made.... Our first bread was made out of corn.

—An early Illinois settler

The Civil War

By the mid–1800s, tensions between the Northern states and Southern states were rising. The Northern states flourished as a result of manufacturing, trade, and mass production. The Southern states thrived by farming cash crops, such as cotton, tobacco, and rice. Southern plantation owners relied on black slaves to raise their crops. Slavery was a basic part of Southern life. As the United States grew, adding new territory in the West, the nation became divided over the issue of slavery. The Northern states were "free states." Slavery had been abolished or was never legal in these states. The free states wanted slavery to be illegal in most of the new states that were added as the nation grew. In addition, some people in the free states opposed slavery on moral grounds. They wanted slavery to be

This illustration shows Abraham Lincoln speaking to a crowd during his campaign for the U.S. Senate in 1858. He lost the race but was elected U.S. president two years later.

abolished throughout the nation.

The Southern states were "slave states." Not only did they consider it a right to own slaves, they also tended to vote together in Congress and did not want to lose power in the national government. To help hold on to their political power, the slave states wanted slavery to be legal in western territories. At the least, they wanted the territories to vote on whether their new state would be a free state or a slave state. In 1861, these differences of opinion blew up. By the spring of 1861, eleven Southern states had broken away from the Union (the United States) and formed the Confederate States of America.

Illinois was a free state. It was one of the twenty-three states that fought for the Union against the Confederacy during the Civil War. More than 250,000 Illinoisans fought in the Union army. Unfortunately, nearly 35,000 of these soldiers died in the war. One Illinois soldier who fought in the war was Ulysses S. Grant. He had volunteered in Springfield, the state's capital, and later rose in rank to become the head of the Union army. A few years later, in 1868, Grant was elected president of the United States.

Abraham Lincoln was a central figure before and during the Civil War. Having studied and practiced law in Illinois, Lincoln set his sights on a political career. While running for the U.S. Senate in 1858, Lincoln participated in many debates in the state. In a number of his debate speeches, he argued against slavery. He

THE LAND OF LINCOLN

Illinoisans are extremely proud that Abraham Lincoln spent most of his adult life in Illinois. Like many people around the world, they admire Lincoln's principles. It is no surprise then that Illinoisans adopted "Land of Lincoln" as the state's slogan.

lost the Senate election, but in 1860, Lincoln was elected president of the United States. He was reelected in 1864.

Lincoln believed that the Union must be held together. He believed that the North had to go to war to force the eleven states that had seceded to rejoin the Union. Lincoln led the country through the Civil War and is often thought of as one of America's greatest leaders. However, he did not get to continue his leadership after the Union victory in the Civil War. On April 14, 1865, only a few days after the main Confederate army surrendered, Lincoln was shot while watching a play in Washington, D.C. He died the next day and was later buried in Springfield, Illinois. A few months after Lincoln's death, the U.S. Constitution was changed. The Thirteenth Amendment officially ended slavery throughout the United States.

Growth and Industrialization

Today, Chicago is one of the largest cities in the United States. But when the first European explorers arrived there in the late 1600s, the site was a swampy area where wild onions and garlic grew. They used an American Indian word, *Checagou*, which, some settlers have written, meant "skunk" or "stink onion."

Chicago's first non–American Indian resident was probably Jean Baptiste Point du Sable. Du Sable was a trader from Haiti who built a small house near the mouth of the Chicago River in the 1780s. The U.S. Army established Fort Dearborn nearby in 1803. Soon European-American settlers started coming to the area. In 1812, Indians attacked and burned Fort Dearborn. The fort was rebuilt four years later, but few people returned to the settlement until the Sauk leader Black Hawk was defeated in the early 1830s. From then on, the city grew rapidly. New canals connected Chicago, along with other growing cities, to the rivers that fed into the Mississippi. Railroads were built across the continent. Many of these train lines met in Chicago. The canals and the railroads helped Chicago become an important port and industrial center in the mid–1800s.

But Chicago almost did not survive into the 1900s. On the night of October 8, 1871, a fire started in or near Patrick and Catherine O'Leary's barn in Chicago and spread through the city. Legend says that a cow kicked over a lantern, but no one knows for sure how the fire started. The Great Chicago Fire destroyed nearly every home and business in the city. Almost 100,000 people were left homeless.

This picture shows the original Fort Dearborn, which was built on the south side of the Chicago River in 1803.

◀ This illustration shows the panic caused by the Great Chicago Fire.

▼ The Historic Water Tower was one of the few large structures that survived the Great Chicago Fire.

More than three hundred people died. Eighteen thousand buildings were destroyed. The people of Chicago fought back, and soon the city was on the rise again. One of the buildings to survive the fire was the Historic Water Tower. It still stands today, surrounded by soaring skyscrapers, and serves as a symbol of Chicago's strong spirit.

New Industries in Illinois

During the 1800s, many new industries were born in Illinois. Cyrus McCormick invented a reaper that helped farmers harvest huge fields of crops quickly. A few years later, John Deere invented a steel plow to replace old wooden and iron plows. The steel plows worked better than wooden ones in the tough prairie soil and lasted longer. Farmers from Illinois and neighboring states sent cattle and

Cyrus McCormick's reaper was a time-saving invention that enabled farmers to harvest wheat faster and grow more crops.

hogs to be slaughtered, or killed, in stockyards near Chicago. Gustavus Swift opened a meat-processing plant in the area. Today, Swift's original company is part of a much larger company that sells food worldwide.

Other industries also got their start in Chicago. Aaron Montgomery Ward began a mail-order business. He was so successful that Richard Sears and Alvah Roebuck did the same thing. Customers from all over the country ordered everything from underwear to water pumps from catalogs that came in the mail. Both companies opened large department stores that generations of shoppers loved to visit. Although Ward's company went out of business after more than 125 years, Sears still has many department stores. With the Internet, today's shoppers can buy from online stores, much as shoppers in the late 1800s ordered goods from catalogs.

Chicago's factories were so successful that by 1890, Illinois was the third-largest manufacturing state in the nation. Illinois was a leader in manufacturing farm machinery, clothing, steel products, food products, and more.

THE GREAT CHICAGO FIRE

Did Mrs. O'Leary's cow really start the Great Chicago Fire? No one knows for sure, but you can make a diorama to illustrate what might have happened.

WHAT YOU NEED

Newspapers or a plastic sheet to protect the table
Shoebox or similar box
Paints and brushes or colored markers
Paper, white and colored
Scissors
Tape and glue
Five or six pipe cleaners
4 ounces (113 grams) of paintable modeling clay—white is best. You can buy special modeling clay in most arts-and-crafts stores or in many toy stores.
Two pennies and a paper clip
A few strands of dry grass
A cotton ball
A pen

Cover the table with newspapers or a plastic sheet.

Stand the box on one long side. Paint one long side on the inside of the box to look like straw. Use paints or markers to decorate the inner walls to look like the inside of a barn or cow stall, with wooden posts and walls. You may want to paint on white paper (measure the paper first) and then tape or glue the paper to the inner walls.

While the paint dries, make a cow and lantern from the modeling clay. For a cow, first twist pipe cleaners into a rough cow shape. The shape can be very simple—four legs, a body, a head, and a tail. Thicken the body with extra pipe cleaners. Then mold modeling clay around this frame. Shape the lantern from modeling clay, too. You might use pennies for the top and bottom and a paper clip (untwisted and reshaped) for a handle. Let the clay dry for twenty-four hours. Paint the cow and lantern when the modeling clay is dry.

Glue dry grass clippings or very thin strips of colored paper, about 2 inches (5 cm) long, to the barn floor. Paint some of the grass (or a spot on the floor) to look like the beginnings of a fire, or glue down some flame-colored paper. Use a wisp of cotton, stiffened with glue, for smoke.

Place the lantern on its side near your "fire." Place the cow nearby. If you like, on one wall, draw a tiny calendar that shows the month the fire began (October 1871). Add any other details you want—such as a milking stool, tools that might be in a barn, or a horse. Use pipe cleaners, modeling clay, and your imagination!

CAUTION: *Do not use any REAL flames in your diorama. You do not want to start a fire of your own!*

Thousands of people gather in Chicago during the Great Depression to protest the tough economic conditions.

Hard Times

In 1914, World War I broke out in Europe. In 1917, the United States entered the war and joined Great Britain and France in fighting Germany. Illinoisans contributed to the war by enlisting in the armed forces and by working in factories to produce war materials. They generally supported the war effort and cut back on expenses to help the nation. It was a difficult time for the country, and more hard times were still to come.

Can you imagine having only a bowl of watery soup as your one meal for the entire day? In the 1930s, many people were lucky to have even that single bowl of soup. The nation had sunk into the Great Depression. Thousands of banks went out of business, and many other businesses failed. Many people lost their farms or their jobs, and some lost their homes. Millions of people across the country were unemployed. It was a time of great hardship. Charles Morgan, who lived in McLean County, Illinois, at the time, said, "Hundreds get scanty [small] allowances through charitys and well fares. Hundreds of acres are gardened by unemployed. Factories are closed. Hardly any one has the cash to buy nessecaries at all. [People are] begging, bartering and trading in different ways to get along."

Another World War

By the end of the 1930s, the world was caught up in World War II. In Europe, Adolf Hitler's Nazi German troops stormed across neighboring countries. In Asia, Japan conquered parts of China and numerous territories that at the time were European colonies. The United States entered the war in 1941, after the Japanese bombed Pearl Harbor, the site of the U.S. naval base in Hawaii.

Factories and farms scrambled to provide supplies needed by the armed forces. Americans worked to make weapons, tanks, trucks, ships, planes, uniforms, and clothing. Though the war brought a great deal of death and misery, it did ease the unemployment of the Great Depression. Thousands of men and women from Illinois served in the armed forces and many more served by working in factories and on farms.

The war brought about great advances in atomic research. In 1942, under the direction of Enrico Fermi, an Italian-American physicist, scientists at the University of Chicago set off the first human-made nuclear chain reaction.

A nuclear chain reaction involves the release of tremendous energy from the nucleus (center) of an atom. Atoms are the building blocks of matter. Research in this area led to the creation of the atomic bomb. The United States dropped two atomic bombs on Japanese cities,

Workers build an airplane engine at a factory in Melrose, Illinois. During World War II, African Americans were permitted to work alongside whites instead of being kept in separate African-American work teams.

which helped bring World War II to an end in 1945. Nuclear research also led to peaceful uses of nuclear power for power plants that make electricity. Today, the Chicago area remains a leader in atomic and nuclear research.

Illinois Today

During the second half of the twentieth century, Illinoisans faced many problems. Increasing costs forced many farmers to sell their land to large corporations or to land developers. Land that was once rich farmland was cleared to make way for homes, businesses, and factories.

Urban areas also faced rough times. During the 1900s, cities had grown increasingly crowded. As a result of the overcrowding, racial tension, poverty, crime, and drug problems increased. By the mid– and late 1900s, many people who could afford to leave moved out of the cities into the expanding suburbs. Many businesses followed the people. The money that the residents and businesses paid in taxes went toward developing the suburban areas. Inner cities had less money to support their schools and for upkeep of older neighborhoods. Inner-city residents also had fewer opportunities to find good jobs.

But Illinoisans today are working hard to solve those problems and create a bright future. Immigrants from all over the world, especially from Latin America and Asia, have moved to Illinois. They are helping to make Illinois a diverse and successful state.

Important Dates

★ **10,000 BCE** Prehistoric hunters live in the area that is now called Illinois.

★ **1673** Marquette and Jolliet explore part of present-day Illinois.

★ **1717** Illinois is incorporated into the French colony of Louisiana.

★ **1763** The French and Indian War between Great Britain and France ends. The British win and claim the area that includes Illinois.

★ **1778** George Rogers Clark captures the fort at Kaskaskia from the British during the American Revolution.

★ **1809** The Illinois Territory is established.

★ **1818** Illinois becomes the nation's twenty-first state.

★ **1832** The Black Hawk War is fought between the Sauk and Fox Indians and Illinois settlers. The Indians are defeated and move westward.

★ **1839** Springfield becomes the state capital.

★ **1847** Cyrus McCormick opens his reaper factory in Chicago.

★ **1860** Abraham Lincoln is elected to his first term as U.S. president.

★ **1861** The Civil War begins.

★ **1865** The Civil War ends. Abraham Lincoln is assassinated.

★ **1871** The Great Chicago Fire destroys most of the city.

★ **1929** The Great Depression begins.

★ **1973** The Sears Tower in Chicago is completed. At the time, it is the world's tallest building. (The building is officially renamed the Willis Tower in 2009.)

★ **1992** Illinois voters elect Carol Moseley-Braun to the U.S. Senate. She becomes the first African-American woman elected to the Senate.

★ **1993** The worst floods in the state's history hit western and southern Illinois.

★ **1997** The Field Museum of Natural History in Chicago spends $8.4 million to acquire "Sue," a nearly complete *Tyrannosaurus rex* skeleton.

★ **2008** Illinois senator Barack Obama is the first African American to be elected president of the United States.

The People

Illinoisans live in cities, suburbs near those cities, country towns, and on farms. They work in a wide variety of jobs. Some people can trace their family history in Illinois back many generations. Others are newcomers to the state.

Farming Life

Farm life in Illinois today is much different from when the first settlers worked to grow crops in the tough sod. Today, most farms are fully computerized, and modern machinery has made farm life easier than it used to be. But farm families still work hard. Children get up about 5:00 A.M. to do chores before getting on the school bus. One young farm boy explained why he likes farming. "[Y]ou can be your own boss," he said. "You can pretty much do what you want from day to day as long as the work gets done."

Illinois farmers and their families are not isolated or behind the times. Today, with computers and Internet connections, people who live in rural areas can enjoy the same benefits of modern life as city people.

From Country Towns to Small Cities

Although more than three-quarters of Illinois is made up of farm fields, most Illinoisans do not live on farms. Towns and small cities are sprinkled throughout the state. Each has its own history, quirks, and culture. Galena in northwestern

Kids take a twirl on a ride at an Illinois amusement park. The people of Illinois have plenty of ways to have fun.

Today, many growers can sell their vegetables and fruits, such as strawberries, at local farmers' markets.

Illinois is a beautiful old historic town. Carbondale calls itself the capital of southern Illinois. A nationally recognized university is located there. Decatur, in the middle of Illinois, is a center for business and industry and an urban hub for the surrounding farming areas. Almost 110,000 people live in and around Decatur. It is one of about a dozen cities in Illinois that are part of a metropolitan area. A metropolitan area has a large central city surrounded by smaller cities or towns.

The biggest metropolitan area in Illinois is the Chicago area. People who live there refer to the city and surrounding suburbs as Chicagoland. Chicago has about 2.8 million people, making it the third-largest city in the country. But the population of the larger Chicago metropolitan area is more than 8 million. In fact, three of Chicago's suburbs—Aurora, Naperville, and Joliet—are among Illinois's six largest cities.

Life In and Around Chicago

Like many large cities, Chicago has interesting restaurants, creative theater, and museums filled with fascinating exhibits. Chicago is also known for its beautiful lakefront and its stunning architecture. It has been named one of the nation's best cities for outdoor adventures. In different seasons, people can go hiking,

PASSION FOR PIZZA

When many food lovers think of Chicago, they think of pizza. The city is famous for its deep-dish-style pizza, with a thick crust and loads of cheese. Legend has it that Ike Sewell invented deep-dish pizza at his restaurant Pizzeria Uno in downtown Chicago in 1943. Today, there are more than two hundred Pizzeria Uno restaurants across the United States.

biking, canoeing, kayaking, swimming, sailing, and cross-country skiing, all in downtown Chicago. Bustling with activity, many parts of Chicago are great places to live and work as well as to visit.

However, not all parts of the city are quite so well-off. In poor neighborhoods, many people have to deal with problems such as high unemployment and crime rates, overcrowding, and poverty. Some public schools in Chicago are very crowded. They do not have enough money to provide textbooks or even teachers for all their students.

To address problems like these, students in some of Chicago's high schools have been working with parents and community groups to improve their education. They did a yearlong study to find out

A school official from Chicago holds a sign at a rally to demand more money for education.

why many students in the local public schools do not complete high school. They visited successful urban schools in other cities to learn effective ways to teach and motivate students. The students produced a report that they presented to the city. Their report outlined how they could work with the community and the school system to help more students graduate from high school and go on to college.

Many of Chicago's suburbs offer the benefits of both a large city and a smaller town. Many people like living in the suburbs because they can live in a quiet and peaceful area but still be close to the liveliness of the city. In fact, five Chicago suburbs have been listed among the best one hundred places to live in the United States. And one of them, Naperville, is almost always near the top of the list.

Diversity in Illinois

As of 2007, the population of Illinois was more than 12.8 million. Only four states had more people. Though more than 70 percent of the population is white, the state's residents come from a wide range of countries and cultures. Illinoisans also come from many different religious backgrounds. The largest religious groups are Protestants and Catholics. The state is also home to many Jews, Muslims, Hindus, Baha'is, and Buddhists. Some Illinoisans choose not to be part of any organized religion.

Quick Facts

NAUVOO

Illinois is important in the history of the Church of Jesus Christ of Latter Day Saints, or the Mormons. In 1839, founder Joseph Smith and his followers settled in Commerce, Illinois. Smith renamed the city Nauvoo. The city's population grew to about 12,000. Still, the Mormons were often persecuted for their beliefs. Smith was murdered in jail in Carthage, Illinois, in June 1844. Less than two years later, Brigham Young led the Mormons out of Nauvoo to a new settlement in Utah. Today, the city of Nauvoo attracts many visitors who come to see historic Mormon sites.

Who Illinoisans Are

Two or More Races
199,006 (1.5%)

Asian
551,835 (4.3%)

Some Other Race
1,132,783 (8.8%)

Black or African American
1,884,069 (14.7%)

White
9,057,076 (70.5%)

American Indian and Alaska Native
21,705 (0.0%)*

Native Hawaiian and Other Pacific Islander
6,074 (0.0%)*

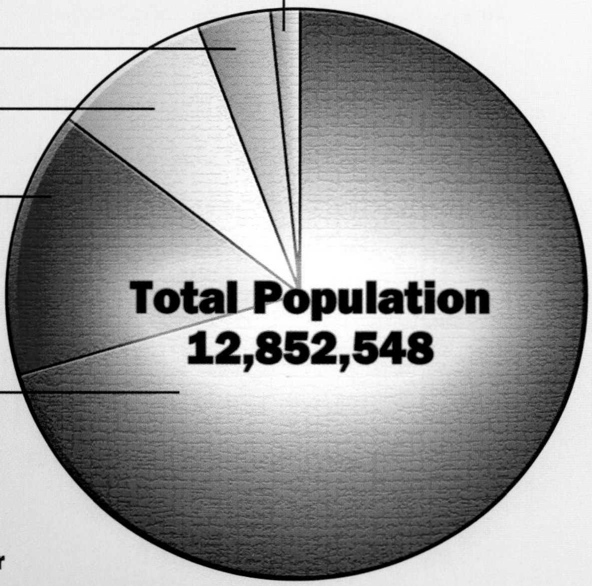

Total Population 12,852,548

Hispanics or Latinos:
- 1,917,420 people
- 14.9% of the state's population

Hispanics or Latinos may be of any race.

Note: The pie chart shows the racial breakdown of the state's population based on the categories used by the U.S. Bureau of the Census. The Census Bureau reports information for Hispanics or Latinos separately, since they may be of any race. Percentages in the pie chart may not add to 100 because of rounding.

* Less than 0.1%.

Source: U.S. Bureau of the Census, 2007 American Community Survey

American Indians

American Indians make up less than one percent of the population of Illinois. Despite their small numbers, American Indians have a strong presence in the state. For decades, they have worked to fight stereotypes and give people accurate information about their different tribes, their cultures, and their traditions. For example, many college athletic teams are named after American Indian tribes or chiefs. Although the team names were not meant to offend anyone, the team symbols and mascots often do fail to show respect for American Indian cultures. American Indians and others at the University of Illinois at Champaign-Urbana brought national attention to this issue. Over the years, many athletic events at the school featured the university mascot, Chief Illiniwek. The mascot would do a dance to raise team spirit. That presented several problems. The Illinois Indians (also called the Illiniwek) were Algonquian. But the mascot's costume was based on the clothing of the Plains Indians. Even more important, traditional dances

Two American Indians carve a totem pole to be displayed at the Field Museum in Chicago.

are sacred rituals in American Indian cultures. They are not meant to entertain crowds at athletic events. Chief Illiniwek's dance offended many people.

In 2007, after numerous meetings with American Indian groups, faculty, students, and alumni, the University of Illinois retired Chief Illiniwek as the school's mascot. The university used the opportunity to educate students about American Indian culture. In 2009, the school invited two leaders of Illinois's Indians to speak on campus. Like many other institutions in Illinois, the university helped bring people of different backgrounds and opinions together to learn from one another.

African Americans in Illinois

The first African-American town to be incorporated in the United States was in Illinois. Brooklyn (in its early years named Lovejoy), Illinois, had its beginnings in the 1820s. Black slaves escaped to the area and set up a community of farmers and craftspeople. Brooklyn, Illinois, was a destination for African Americans for decades.

Today, most African Americans in Illinois do not live in small towns like Brooklyn. More than 97 percent of the state's African Americans live in urban areas. Since the early 1900s, they have formed aid organizations to promote education and help people find jobs. The Urban League is one example. Today, Chicago, Springfield, and Peoria have very active Urban League chapters that continue to improve life for people in these cities.

African Americans in Illinois have formed other organizations to help children and families make good lives for themselves. In Chicago and Rockford, the organization 100 Black Men coordinates mentoring and other programs for African-American children, especially young boys. A mentor is an older or more experienced person who works one-on-one with a younger person and acts as a role model. Members of 100 Black Men groups generally have successful careers. When they meet with students, they talk about things that have helped them set and reach their goals: self-respect, taking responsibility, being part of a healthy community, and education.

Many African-American Illinoisans have made significant contributions to the arts. Gwendolyn Brooks was the first African-American poet to win a Pulitzer Prize—a major award for authors, poets, journalists, and music composers. Miles Davis (jazz), Mahalia Jackson (gospel), and Muddy Waters (the blues) each helped popularize a different style of music and, in doing so, enriched American culture. Music producer Quincy Jones helped create many famous recordings, including Michael Jackson's *Thriller* album.

Popular talk show host Oprah Winfrey gained her fame in Chicago. She has used her show to influence people in many positive ways. Oprah has also used her wealth and power to start charities and to highlight problems in society. With Oprah's Book Club, she has promoted reading and helped sell millions of books.

Superstar Derrick Rose of the Chicago Bulls teaches kids at a basketball clinic in 2009.

Famous Illinoisans

Jane Addams: Social Reformer

Jane Addams was an important early social reformer. Born in Cedarville, Illinois, in 1860, she went on to cofound Chicago's Hull House in 1889. Hull House was a settlement house, where immigrants could take classes and get help adjusting to their new lives. Addams spoke out against child labor and worked for world peace. Jane Addams Hull House continues to serve Chicagoans today.

Walt Disney: Entertainment Producer

Born in Chicago in 1901, Walt Disney went on to create Mickey Mouse and many other much-loved cartoon characters. He also produced classic feature-length animated films, such as *Snow White and the Seven Dwarfs* and *Cinderella*. He won

more than thirty Academy Awards—the top awards for films—for his work. Disney died in 1966, but his spirit lives on in the wonderful characters he created and in the Disney theme parks and film and television studios.

Gwendolyn Brooks: Poet

Gwendolyn Brooks was born in Kansas in 1917, but she grew up in Chicago. Many of her poems are about the experiences of African Americans. Famous throughout the United States, she was appointed Poet Laureate of Illinois in 1968. She died in Chicago in 2000, at the age of 83.

Miles Davis: Musician

Born in Alton, Illinois, in 1926, Miles Davis became a world-famous trumpet player, bandleader, and composer. Many consider him to be one of the most influential jazz musicians in history.

Sandra Cisneros: Writer

Sandra Cisneros, born in 1954, set her first book in the Chicago neighborhood where she grew up. *The House on Mango Street* is a best-seller, read in many classrooms. Cisneros likes to encourage other writers. She has set up a foundation that gives a yearly writing award, and she meets with other writers to work for à better world.

Barack Obama: Politician

Barack Obama was born in Hawaii in 1961. As a young man in the mid–1980s, he worked in Chicago as a community organizer. After graduating from Harvard Law School in Massachusetts, he returned to Chicago, and he was later elected to the Illinois state senate. In 2004, Obama won a seat in the U.S. Senate, and in 2008, he was elected the forty-fourth president of the United States.

Other Large Ethnic Groups

Over the past thirty years, many immigrants have moved to Illinois. For example, since the early 1980s, thousands of people from Eastern Europe have come to the state. In fact, Chicago, which has a large Polish-American population, claims to be the world's largest "Polish city" outside Poland.

Large numbers of people from Latin America and Asia have also moved to Illinois in recent decades. The U.S. Census Bureau estimates that by 2015 Illinois will have more than 2 million people of Hispanic descent and almost 750,000 people of Asian descent.

Hispanic Americans come to Illinois from many different places: Mexico, Puerto Rico, Venezuela, El Salvador, Colombia, and Guatemala, to name just a few. Asian Americans also come from a wide variety of countries, including India, the Philippines, China, South Korea, Vietnam, and Japan. No matter where they were born or where in Illinois they decide to live, immigrants often play an important part in shaping their communities. In larger towns and cities, some immigrants open stores and restaurants that sell their native foods and goods. Other immigrants work for—or establish—some of the thousands of businesses that are vital to the state's economy.

The growth of immigrant populations can cause some problems, however. One of the biggest is tensions with residents who do not welcome the changes in their communities that newcomers often bring. For some immigrants, not knowing the English language or American customs can prevent them from succeeding at work or in school. Some immigrants have faced prejudice and discrimination simply because they are seen as "different."

One way government and businesses in Illinois help meet the needs of immigrant communities is by promoting businesses run by minorities. For the past few years, the state has held an event called the Heart of Illinois Trade Fair to showcase such businesses. In addition, national industries often hold conventions in Chicago and other Illinois cities. These conventions provide more opportunities for local minority businesses owners. At such conventions, business owners can meet other business owners in Illinois and elsewhere. Making connections like these benefits the state's economy and also strengthens feelings of community.

A street vendor sells tamales in front of a Mexican-American grocery store in Chicago.

Calendar of Events

★ Old Settlers Days

Every April, at Red Hills State Park, visitors can see what life was like for the pioneers of early Illinois.

★ Kids Day

This gathering for children at Cahokia Mounds each May features games, storytelling, pottery making, and many other activities to honor the state's American Indian heritage.

★ Migration Celebration

In May, the Cypress Creek National Wildlife Refuge in Ullin has activities related to bird migrations, including photography workshops and hiking.

★ Harvard Milk Days

This festival, held in the beginning of June, brings thousands of people to the city of Harvard to celebrate dairy farming. Attractions include farm tours, cattle and horse shows, an arts-and-crafts fair, a parade, and a carnival.

★ General Grierson Liberty Days

One of the largest Civil War reenactments and exhibitions in the Midwest is held every June in Jacksonville.

★ Mid-American Canoe Race

Every June, people gather to race their canoes and kayaks from St. Charles or Batavia to Aurora.

★ Kickapoo Powwow

Every June in LeRoy, American Indian tribes gather to celebrate their heritage. Visitors watch performances of traditional dances, try different types of foods, and enjoy crafts and other activities.

★ Superman Celebration

In June, many people gather for this annual festival in Superman's "hometown" of Metropolis.

★ Heart of Illinois Fair

Illinois's official state fair is held in Peoria and lasts for nine days in July.

★ Taste of Chicago

Every summer, Chicago hosts the largest outdoor food festival in the world. Millions of people sample food from area restaurants and listen to live music from well-known artists.

★ Broom Corn Festival

The people of Arcola, the "Broom Corn Capital of the World," take to the streets each September with broom activities, arts and crafts, parades, and entertainment. Broomcorn is a grasslike plant used to make brooms and brushes.

★ Fort Crevecoeur Annual Rendezvous

Every September, this event re-creates the fur-trading era.

How the Government Works

I llinois, like all states, has different levels of government. Individual villages, towns, and cities have their own local government. People in cities, towns, and villages generally elect a mayor and council members to be in charge locally. County government makes up a higher level of local government. A county usually includes a number of villages or towns and sometimes a larger city. Each of Illinois's 102 counties is divided into districts. Each district elects one supervisor (sometimes called a commissioner) to the board of supervisors that governs the county.

The state government is centered in Illinois's capital city, Springfield. The state government has a structure much like that of the federal (national) government. The U.S. Constitution describes the structure and basic rules for the federal government. Similarly, the Illinois constitution describes the structure and rules of the state government. The state government is divided into the executive branch, the legislative branch, and the judicial branch.

Governing Illinois

A governor of a state is similar to the president of the nation. He or she is usually considered the most important figure in the government. Illinois voters elect their governor to a four-year term. While in office, the governor is in charge of approving the state's budget. The governor also works with citizens, businesses,

A bronze statue of Abraham Lincoln stands in front of the State Capitol in Springfield.

Branches of Government

EXECUTIVE ★ ★ ★ ★ ★ ★ ★ ★
The executive branch enforces the state's laws and runs the state government. The governor, who is elected to a four-year term, heads the executive branch.

LEGISLATIVE ★ ★ ★ ★ ★ ★ ★ ★
The Illinois legislature, called the General Assembly, makes the state's laws. The General Assembly has two houses, both of which must pass a bill before it can become a law. One house, the senate, has 59 members, who are elected to two-year or four-year terms. The other house, called the house of representatives, has 118 members, all of whom are elected to two-year terms.

JUDICIAL ★ ★ ★ ★ ★ ★ ★ ★
The judicial branch contains the state's courts. Those courts apply the state's laws in specific cases and decide whether laws agree with the state constitution and are being enforced fairly. The Illinois supreme court is the state's highest court. It hears cases that are appealed from lower courts. The state supreme court has seven justices, who are elected to ten-year terms.

and state agencies to help Illinoisans have a high quality of life. To that end, every year the governor makes a speech often called "the State of the State" address. In the speech, the governor talks about Illinois's successes and how to continue them. He or she also discusses problems affecting the state and proposes ways to fix them.

Illinois's constitution calls for the election of five other members of the executive branch and describes their duties. The lieutenant governor assists the governor and will take over if the governor cannot complete his or her term. The attorney general is the top lawyer for Illinois. He or she helps decide legal matters that are important to the state and its citizens. The treasurer is in charge of the investment and safekeeping of the state's money. The comptroller keeps financial accounts for the state. The secretary of state is in charge of all recordkeeping for Illinois, including driver's licenses and other licenses.

Illinois's legislature is the General Assembly. It is made up of the Illinois house of representatives and the Illinois senate. The voters of Illinois elect members to the house every two years. As for the senators, some are elected to serve for four years and others for two years. Each citizen is represented by a member in each body of the General Assembly. So every Illinoisan has one state senator and one state representative. The General Assembly members are the lawmakers for the state.

Illinois's judicial branch has three levels. The circuit courts are the state's lower-level courts. Circuit courts hear cases that involve possible violation of state civil or criminal laws. Circuit-court decisions can be appealed to a state appellate court. The highest of the state courts is the Illinois supreme court.

Two men walk across an eye-catching floor at the James R. Thompson Center in Chicago. A number of important state government agencies are based in the center. It is named after former Illinois governor Thompson, who served from 1977 to 1991.

U.S. president Barack Obama served in the Illinois state senate from 1997 to 2004.

The state supreme court makes judgments related to appeals of important cases, especially cases of interpreting the law.

In Illinois, the main judges are elected for all the state's courts. However, judges in the circuit court can appoint associate judges to help them hear cases. Illinois's supreme- and appellate-court judges are elected for ten-year terms. Circuit-court judges are elected for six-year terms. Associate-judge appointments are four-year terms.

A meeting room in the State Capitol has desktop voting machines that legislators use to cast votes.

In Washington, D.C.

Like all other states, Illinois is represented in the U.S. Congress in Washington, D.C. Illinois voters elect two U.S. senators who serve six-year terms. In 2010, Illinois had nineteen representatives in the U.S. House of Representatives. Representatives serve two-year terms. A state's population determines its number of representatives.

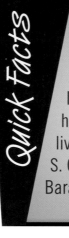

Quick Facts

PRESIDENTS FROM ILLINOIS
Four presidents were born in Illinois or called the state their home for key parts of their adult lives: Abraham Lincoln, Ulysses S. Grant, Ronald Reagan, and Barack Obama.

Contacting Lawmakers

★ ★ ★ ★ ★ ★ ★ ★ ★ ★ ★ ★ ★

Here are some websites you can visit if you want to contact any member of Illinois's General Assembly.

Use any Illinois street address or zip code to find the names of the lawmakers who represent the people living in that area.

http://www.elections.illinois.gov/ DistrictLocator/SELECTSEARCHTYPE. ASPX

If you know the names of legislators or their district numbers, you can get contact information for them and find out about committees they are on and bills they have proposed.

To find information on Illinois state senators, visit:

http://www.ilga.gov/senate

To find information on Illinois state representatives, visit:

http://www.ilga.gov/house

How a Bill Becomes a Law

Did you ever wonder how state laws are passed? You might be surprised to find that any citizen can get it all started. If a person or a group of people think that a new law needs to be passed, they might circulate a petition. A petition is a formal written request that is signed by people who want the request carried out. The petition describes how the signers would like the state to deal with their issue. It may suggest wording for a new law. When the petition has hundreds of signatures, the people circulating the petition send it to their representatives in the Illinois house and senate.

The legislators in Springfield gauge public interest in the issue. If they receive a lot of phone calls, e-mails, letters, or petitions about it, they might work with their staff and other legislators to draft, or write, a bill. A bill is a proposal for a new law.

Legislators work together to present the bill in the General Assembly. The bill goes through several steps before it becomes a law. Separately, in both the house and the senate, legislators review, debate, and often rewrite and amend the bill.

Illinois governor Pat Quinn holds a law that he signed in January 2009. The new law created a commission to fight corruption in government.

In the process, the bill is read aloud and voted on three times in the house and three times in the senate. The bill has to pass by a simple majority each time it comes up in both bodies of the legislature.

Often, even when both the senate and the house pass a bill, the versions that the two houses pass are not exactly the same. So senators and representatives form a committee to combine the two versions into one final bill. The new bill must again pass in both bodies of the legislature. If the final bill is passed by both houses of the General Assembly, it goes to the governor. If the governor approves the bill, it becomes a new state law. If the governor vetoes, or rejects, the bill, it is sent back to the General Assembly. The legislature has another chance to vote on the bill. If both the house and the senate pass the bill by a three-fifths majority, the bill becomes a new law.

Making a Living

How do people in Illinois earn their living? Some fields include agriculture, natural resources, business, industrial and engineering technology, arts and communications, and health care.

Agriculture

Agriculture has always been a key part of Illinois's economy. Early European-American settlers found Illinois to be an excellent place for both grazing animals and growing crops. An article in an 1843 Illinois newspaper quoted one person who said, "Thousands of hogs was raised without any expense." Another article in the same publication spoke of "the ease with which [corn] is cultivated."

In the pioneer days, most people made their living on small farms. Today, less than one percent of Illinoisans work on farms, but the state is still the nation's second-largest producer of corn and soybeans. It is also the country's fourth-largest producer of hogs.

Unlike the small family-run farms of long ago, today's farms are part of a highly specialized industry. Many farmers hold university degrees and use scientific and technological knowledge to make their farms as productive as possible. Illinois farmers provide food and food products for people in their own state and other states. Over the years, Illinois's farm crop exports have also been increasing in value. Exports are products that people sell to other countries.

Vacationers enjoy tubing on one of Illinois's many waterways. Tourism is big business in the state.

An Illinois farmer and his children examine their wheat crop.

In recent decades, many Illinois farmers who live close to a city have sold their land. Most of the time, the land is no longer used for farms. Instead, homes, businesses, and factories have been built in their place. However, in the past few years, the value of Illinois farmland has gone up dramatically. Many people realize that in addition to being important for producing food, fertile farmland can be a great investment.

Many Illinoisans who do not work directly on a farm still depend on Illinois agriculture for their jobs. Food-related industries include grain and flour milling, manufacturing food for farm animals and pets, meat processing and packing, and producing processed and packaged foods. These industries are very important to the state's economy. In fact, Chicago is one of the world's leading cities for processing, packaging, and distributing food products.

RECIPE FOR CORN CHOWDER

Illinois farms are well known for their corn, which is used in desserts, breads, soups, and other delicious dishes. Follow this recipe to make a warm and tasty batch of corn chowder. You will need to use the stove, so ask an adult for help before you get started.

WHAT YOU NEED

2 potatoes, peeled and cut into small chunks

$\frac{3}{4}$ cup (180 milliliters) water

2 $\frac{1}{2}$ cups (595 ml) milk

$\frac{1}{2}$ teaspoon (2 $\frac{1}{2}$ ml) salt

2 cans whole corn kernels

2 cans cream-style corn

Place the potatoes in a medium saucepan and cover with water. Boil until soft.

Drain the potatoes and transfer them to a large pot. Add the $\frac{3}{4}$ cup water, milk, salt, and cans of corn.

Cook the soup mixture over low to medium heat until it simmers. Remove the chowder from the stove, let it cool until it can be safely eaten, and enjoy!

Manufacturing and Construction

Until the 1980s, thousands of people in the cities of Illinois worked in steel mills or factories that manufactured farm, construction, and industrial machinery; transportation equipment; and chemicals.

However, over the past few decades, costs of labor and benefits for workers have gone up. Many business owners moved their factories to other countries, where labor was much cheaper. Other factories closed because their buildings and equipment were old and the cost of replacing them was too high. When manufacturing plants closed in Illinois, many people lost their jobs. Many Illinoisans who work in construction and related industries have lost jobs in recent years because of the economic problems that hit the entire country.

A worker helps assemble a new car at a Ford manufacturing plant in Chicago.

Workers & Industries

Industry	Number of People Working in That Industry	Percentage of All Workers Who Are Working in That Industry
Education and health care	1,267,793	20.5%
Wholesale and retail businesses	901,720	14.6%
Manufacturing	830,516	13.4%
Publishing, media, entertainment, hotels, and restaurants	673,868	10.9%
Professionals, scientists, and managers	649,948	10.5%
Banking and finance, insurance, and real estate	488,648	7.9%
Construction	407,028	6.6%
Transportation and public utilities	383,042	6.2%
Other services	285,726	4.6%
Government	230,837	3.7%
Farming, fishing, forestry, and mining	64,623	1.0%
Totals	**6,183,749**	**100%**

Notes: Figures above do not include people in the armed forces. "Professionals" includes people such as doctors and lawyers. Percentages may not add to 100 because of rounding.

Source: U.S. Bureau of the Census, 2007 estimates

Even so, both manufacturing and construction are still very important industries in Illinois. In addition to food-manufacturing industries, Illinois is home to many other manufacturing businesses, which create a wide variety of products. Some companies make heavy machinery. Others make electronics, computers, and computer parts. Some firms specialize in items made from plastics. Other companies make objects from cement, concrete, and recycled steel that are used in the construction industry. The state also has paper mills, printers, and publishers. Some companies make medicines, and others make medical instruments. Still, Illinois's biggest manufacturing industry is the chemical industry. Among other products, Illinois chemical manufacturers make fertilizers, ethanol (an automobile fuel), and even chemicals for cleaning polluted water. With all these different kinds of factories, Illinois ranks fifth in the nation as a manufacturing state.

Services, Sales, and Entertainment

More than half of Illinois workers are employed in a service industry. Service industries are those whose main business is helping people: hospitals, schools, insurance agencies, governmental agencies, banks and other financial institutions, hotels, retail stores, and restaurants are a few examples.

Chicago is the financial center of the Midwest. In fact, the U.S. government has a bank there: the Federal Reserve Bank of Chicago. Chicago also has a stock exchange, similar to the New York Stock Exchange on Wall Street. The Chicago

SHOPPING IN DOWNTOWN CHICAGO

Downtown Chicago is a shopper's paradise. It has huge department stores and tiny boutiques. Shoppers find everything from wholesale diamonds to building tools in the State Street shopping district. The glittery shops and high fashion along the Magnificent Mile on North Michigan Avenue draw people from around the world.

Mercantile Exchange and the Chicago Board of Options Exchange also play important roles in worldwide investment.

Chicago, along with other cities in Illinois, helps make the state a center for wholesale and retail trade. The state's central location and its strong transportation system help link Illinois to the rest of the country and the world.

Illinois's professional sports teams bring a lot of money to the state. Chicago has two famous baseball teams, the Cubs and the White Sox. The Chicago Blackhawks are one of the oldest professional hockey teams. The city's football and basketball teams, the Bears and the Bulls, have fans all over the country. The Chicago Fire, a Major League Soccer team, also have a loyal following. In addition,

Wrigley Field has been home to the Chicago Cubs since 1914. It is the second-oldest stadium in Major League Baseball after Fenway Park in Boston.

fans of auto racing flock to Chicagoland Speedway in Joliet to watch their favorite NASCAR and IndyCar drivers.

Tourism is also an important part of Illinois's economy. Tourists from all over the world come to see everything that Illinois has to offer. They may want to see the bustling city of Chicago, the beautiful blue waters of Lake Michigan, or the wilderness in Shawnee National Forest. Tourists and residents alike enjoy kayaking, rock climbing, fishing, and camping in Illinois's many and varied state parks and natural areas. The money that tourists spend in hotels, restaurants, and shops helps boost the economy of the Prairie State.

Education

Education is very important in Illinois—and a big part of the economy. As of 2009, the state had close to 5,500 elementary and secondary schools and more than 2.3 million students in grades pre-K through 12. Public and nonpublic schools in the state employ about 200,000 people.

The University of Illinois has campuses in Chicago, Springfield, and Urbana-Champaign. More than 70,000 students are enrolled on the three campuses, and thousands more take classes off campus and online. Illinois operates eight other public universities that are scattered throughout the state.

In Their Own Words

I've been fortunate to go to some of the top schools in America ... but I can tell you, without a doubt, that some of the best lessons I've learned in life are from playing basketball on Chicago's inner-city playgrounds.

—Arne Duncan, U.S. Secretary of Education

Illinois also has many fine private colleges and universities. The University of Chicago is one of the leading research centers in the country. Some of the top scholars and scientists in the world have taught at or attended the university. U.S. president Barack Obama was a professor at the University of Chicago Law School for twelve years before he was elected to the U.S. Senate. Northwestern University in Evanston is another private university with a top reputation throughout the country. Its graduates include many well-known politicians, business leaders, entertainers, and journalists.

Scientists monitor part of a high-tech particle accelerator at Fermilab in Batavia, Illinois. Experts from the University of Chicago do advanced scientific research at the lab.

HAMBURGER U.

Illinois is home to one of the country's more unusual schools of higher learning. Since 1961, thousands of future McDonald's restaurant owners and managers have graduated from Hamburger University in Oak Brook. McDonald's world headquarters is also located in the Chicago suburb.

Products & Resources

Fluorite

Fluorite is needed for the manufacture of glass, steel, and many chemicals. Fluorite is the state mineral because Illinois used to have the most productive fluorite mines in the United States. Today, however, most of the nation's supply of this mineral comes from other countries.

Corn

Illinois's yearly harvest of more than 2 billion bushels of corn makes it the country's second-largest producer of this important crop. Each year, more than 250 million bushels of Illinois corn are used to produce ethanol. When mixed with gasoline, ethanol is used to fuel cars and trucks. Illinois produces more than 650 million gallons (2.5 trillion liters) of ethanol—more than any other state.

Soybeans

Soybeans have been an important crop in China for thousands of years. However, farmers in Illinois started planting soybeans only in the mid–1850s. Today, Illinois is among the top soybean producers in the world. The state exports thousands of bushels to China and other countries in Asia every year. Soybeans are also used in making biodiesel fuel. Unlike the oil that is used to make gasoline, biodiesel is a renewable fuel. The soybeans used for biodiesel can be grown as a crop year after year.

Steel

In years past, steel production was an important Illinois industry. Illinois still has some steel mills, including some mini mills that recycle iron and steel to produce new products.

Dairy Farming

Illinois dairy farms provide fresh milk, cheese, and other dairy products. These products are shipped throughout the state and to other states as well.

Transportation

Chicago's O'Hare Airport is one of the world's busiest airports. Each day, thousands of people and hundreds of tons of products fly in and out of O'Hare. Cars and trucks travel through Illinois on its many highways, and boats and barges make their way on the state's waterways.

Visitors learn about Illinois's long history of coal mining at an exhibit at Chicago's Museum of Science and Industry.

Coal Mining and Energy Production

Illinois needs a lot of electricity to power its homes and businesses. But electricity production is important in Illinois for another reason. The state makes money by exporting some of the electricity it generates to other states.

Today, nuclear power plants provide more than half the electricity generated in Illinois. However, the nuclear power plants in Illinois and across the country are several decades old. They will need to be rebuilt or replaced soon. The state of Illinois is looking at new ways to provide energy. Many Illinoisans would like to find new, cleaner ways of using coal as a fuel in power plants. They are also looking for ways to use coal instead of petroleum-based fuels.

Coal mining was once one of Illinois's most important industries. Coal lies below more than 65 percent of Illinois, yet very little coal is mined in the state. Why? Illinois coal contains large amounts of sulfur. When the coal is burned, it releases a gas called sulfur dioxide. Sulfur dioxide is a serious pollutant that is harmful to people, animals, and plants.

The technology for reducing the amount of sulfur dioxide released when coal is burned has been available since the 1990s. Yet Illinois coal has remained in low demand. Burning coal causes another environmental problem. It releases a lot of carbon dioxide gas into the air and contributes to global warming—the slow rise in worldwide temperatures.

In recent years, scientists have developed new technologies related to burning coal. Using these technologies, factories and power plants that burn coal can capture the carbon dioxide that is released. Not only does this reduce air pollution, but it may actually help the coal-burning power plants make more money. They can sell purified carbon dioxide to other businesses, such as oil companies that pump it into their wells to keep the oil flowing.

The Environment and Conservation

Illinoisans know that it is important to protect the air we breathe, the water we drink, our natural resources, and our wildlife. The state has developed many programs to encourage people to protect the environment. Some of these programs encourage the use of renewable energy sources, such as solar and wind power.

Like all renewable resources, wind will never run out. Illinois has a program to help people learn about wind energy. The state makes maps

The wind spins the giant blades of a wind turbine in northeastern Illinois. Wind energy is a growing industry in Illinois—and the rest of the country.

that show people how windy it is where they live. They can use the maps to decide whether installing a wind turbine would help them save money on their electricity bill. People who produce more electricity than they use might even be able to make money by selling their extra electricity back to one of Illinois's power companies.

Most schools in Illinois have special environmental awareness programs. Earth Day in the Park is held at state parks around Illinois each spring. Students at these events may plant trees, restore a local prairie, or even help build a butterfly garden. They enjoy coming back later in the year to see how their project has helped the environment.

Looking to the Future

Illinois will continue to grow and change. New industries will replace old ones. Cities will grow and change as populations shift. But the spirit of the people and their ability to adapt have helped Illinois get through difficult times. Its proud people are ready to face the future. It is their enthusiasm that has kept the Prairie State alive and well.

State Flag & Seal

Illinois's flag shows the state seal on a white background.

The state seal has a bald eagle holding a shield with the stars and stripes that represent the thirteen original states. In its beak, the eagle holds a banner with the state's motto—State Sovereignty, National Union. The eagle is perched on a boulder that shows the year the state entered the Union (1818) and the year this version of the seal was adopted (1868).

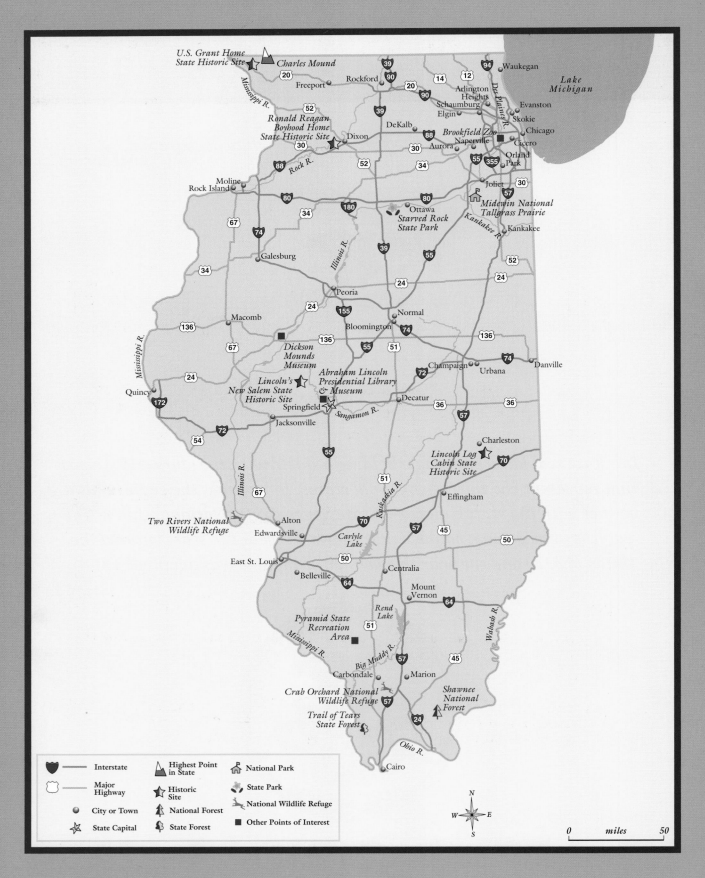

U.S. Grant Home
State Historic Site
Charles Mound

Mississippi R.

20

Freeport

39

Rockford

90

20

14

12

94

Waukegan

Lake
Michigan

Arlington
Heights
Schaumburg
Elgin

Des Plaines R.

Evanston
Skokie
Chicago

52

39

DeKalb

Ronald Reagan
Boyhood Home
State Historic Site

30

Dixon

88

Aurora

Naperville

Brookfield Zoo

Cicero

Orland
Park

30

Moline
Rock Island

88

Rock R.

52

34

55

355

80

34

80

Joliet

57

Midewin National
Tallgrass Prairie

67

74

180

Ottawa

Starved Rock
State Park

Kankakee R.

30

Kankakee

Galesburg

Illinois R.

39

55

52

34

24

24

Macomb

136

24

Peoria

155

Normal

74

136

Bloomington

74

Danville

67

Dickson
Mounds
Museum

136

55

51

72

Champaign

Urbana

136

Quincy

67

24

Lincoln's
New Salem State
Historic Site

Abraham Lincoln
Presidential Library
& Museum

Decatur

36

36

172

Springfield

Sangamon R.

57

Charleston

54

72

Jacksonville

Lincoln Log
Cabin State
Historic Site

70

Illinois R.

55

51

Effingham

67

Two Rivers National
Wildlife Refuge

Alton

Edwardsville

70

Kaskaskia R.

57

45

50

Carlyle
Lake

East St. Louis

50

Centralia

Belleville

64

Mount
Vernon

64

Wabash R.

Pyramid State
Recreation
Area

51

Rend
Lake

Mississippi R.

57

45

Big Muddy R.

Carbondale

Marion

Shawnee
National
Forest

Crab Orchard National
Wildlife Refuge

57

Trail of Tears
State Forest

24

Ohio R.

Cairo

Interstate

Major
Highway

City or Town

State Capital

Highest Point
in State

Historic
Site

National Forest

State Forest

National Park

State Park

National Wildlife Refuge

Other Points of Interest

N
W   E
S

0   miles   50

76 ILLINOIS

State Song

Illinois

words by C.H. Chamberlain
music by Archibald Johnston

BOOKS

Bial, Raymond. *Nauvoo: Mormon City on the Mississippi River*. Boston: Houghton Mifflin, 2006.

Fradin, Judith, and Dennis Fradin. *Jane Addams: Champion of Democracy*. New York: Clarion Books, 2006.

Horn, Geoffrey M. *Barack Obama*. Pleasantville, NY: Gareth Stevens, 2009.

Hurd, Owen. *Chicago History for Kids: Triumphs and Tragedies of the Windy City*. Chicago: Chicago Review Press, 2007.

Nobleman, Marc Tyler. *The Great Chicago Fire*. Minneapolis, MN: Compass Point Books, 2006.

Pauketat, Timothy, and Nancy Stone. *Cahokia Mounds*. New York: Oxford University Press, 2004.

WEBSITES

Illinois State Historical Library:
http://www.state.il.us/HPA/PrairiePages.htm

Official Illinois State Website:
http://www.state.il.us

Official Illinois State Tourism Website:
http://www.enjoyillinois.com

Claire Price-Groff is the author of several books for young adults. She particularly loves writing about history and the people who made it. Some of her books are *Extraordinary Women Journalists*, *Twentieth-Century Women Political Leaders*, *The Manatee*, *Great Conquerors*, *The Importance of Queen Elizabeth I*, and *Queen Victoria and Nineteenth-Century England*.

Elizabeth Kaplan has edited textbooks and reference works on a wide variety of subjects. She is also the author of several science and social studies books for young adults. Throughout her life, Kaplan has enjoyed going on road trips. In her travels, she has been to forty-seven of the fifty states. Kaplan grew up in Illinois, which she still visits frequently. She lives with her husband and two daughters in southeastern Wisconsin.

Page numbers in **boldface** are illustrations.